Your Government:
How It Works

The Impeachment Process

Pegi Deitz Shea

Arthur M. Schlesinger, jr.
Senior Consulting Editor

Chelsea House Publishers
Philadelphia

CHELSEA HOUSE PUBLISHERS
Editor in Chief Stephen Reginald
Production Manager Pamela Loos
Art Director Sara Davis
Director of Photography Judy L. Hasday
Managing Editor James D. Gallagher
Senior Production Editor LeeAnne Gelletly

Staff for THE IMPEACHMENT PROCESS
Project Editor/Publishing Coordinator Jim McAvoy
Associate Art Director Takeshi Takahashi
Series Designer Takeshi Takahashi, Keith Trego

The Chelsea House World Wide Web address is
http://www.chelseahouse.com

3 5 7 9 8 6 4 2

Library of Congress Cataloging-in-Publication Data

Shea, Pegi Deitz.
    The impeachment process: by Pegi Deitz Shea.
        p. cm. — (Your government—how it works)
    Includes bibliographical references and index.
    Summary: Analyzes the Constitution's provision for impeach-
ment and chronicles how this law has been used throughout
American history to remove elected officials from power.
    ISBN 0-7910-5538-8 (hc)
    1. Impeachments—United States—Juvenile literature. 2. Presi-
dents—United States—Juvenile literature. [1. Impeachments.
2. United States—Politics and government.] I. Title. II. Series.
    KF5075.Z9 S53 2000
    342.73'062—dc21   99-048607

Contents

YOUR GOVERNMENT HOW IT WORKS

Introduction

Government: Crises of Confidence

Arthur M. Schlesinger, jr.

FROM THE START, Americans have regarded their government with a mixture of reliance and mistrust. The men who founded the republic understood the importance of government. "If men were angels," observed the 51st Federalist Paper, "no government would be necessary." But men are not angels. Because human beings are subject to wicked as well as to noble impulses, government was deemed essential to assure freedom and order.

The American revolutionaries, however, also knew that government could become a source of injury and oppression. The men who gathered in Philadelphia in 1787 to write the Constitution therefore had two purposes in mind: They wanted to establish a strong central authority and to limit that central authority's capacity to abuse its power.

To prevent the abuse of power, the Founding Fathers wrote two basic principles into the Constitution. The principle of federalism divided power between the state governments and the central authority. The principle of the separation of powers subdivided the central authority itself into three branches—the executive, the legislative, and the judiciary—so that "each may be a check on the other."

YOUR GOVERNMENT: HOW IT WORKS examines some of the major parts of that central authority, the federal government. It explains how various officials, agencies, and departments operate and explores the political organizations that have grown up to serve the needs of government.

Introduction

The federal government as presented in the Constitution was more an idealistic construct than a practical administrative structure. It was barely functional when it came into being.

This was especially true of the executive branch. The Constitution did not describe the executive branch in any detail. After vesting executive power in the president, it assumed the existence of "executive departments" without specifying what these departments should be. Congress began defining their functions in 1789 by creating the Departments of State, Treasury, and War.

President Washington, assisted by Secretary of the Treasury Alexander Hamilton, equipped the infant republic with a working administrative structure. Congress also continued that process by creating more executive departments as they were needed.

Throughout the 19th century, the number of federal government workers increased at a consistently faster rate than did the population. Increasing concerns about the politicization of public service led to efforts—bitterly opposed by politicians—to reform it in the latter part of the century.

The 20th century saw considerable expansion of the federal establishment. More importantly, it saw growing impatience with bureaucracy in society as a whole.

The Great Depression during the 1930s confronted the nation with its greatest crisis since the Civil War. Under Franklin Roosevelt, the New Deal reshaped the federal government, assigning it a variety of new responsibilities and greatly expanding its regulatory functions. By 1940, the number of federal workers passed the 1 million mark.

Critics complained of big government and bureaucracy. Business owners resented federal regulation. Conservatives worried about the impact of paternalistic government on self-reliance, on community responsibility, and on economic and personal freedom.

When the United States entered World War II in 1941, government agencies focused their energies on supporting the war effort. By the end of World War II, federal civilian employment had risen to 3.8 million. With peace, the federal establishment declined to around 2 million in 1950. Then growth resumed, reaching 2.8 million by the 1980s.

A large part of this growth was the result of the national government assuming new functions such as: affirmative action in civil rights, environmental protection, and safety and health in the workplace.

Some critics became convinced that the national government was a steadily growing behemoth swallowing up the liberties of the people. The 1980s brought new intensity to the debate about government growth. Foes of Washington bureaucrats preferred local government, feeling it more responsive to popular needs.

But local government is characteristically the government of the locally powerful. Historically, the locally powerless have often won their human and constitutional rights by appealing to the national government. The national government has defended racial justice against local bigotry, upheld the Bill of Rights against local vigilantism, and protected natural resources from local greed. It has civilized industry and secured the rights of labor organizations. Had the states' rights creed prevailed, perhaps slavery would still exist in the United States.

Americans are still of two minds. When pollsters ask large, spacious questions—Do you think government has become too involved in your lives? Do you think government should stop regulating business?—a sizable majority opposes big government. But when asked specific questions about the practical work of government—Do you favor Social Security? Unemployment compensation? Medicare? Health and safety standards in factories? Environmental protection?—a sizable majority approves of intervention.

We do not like bureaucracy, but we cannot live without it. We need its genius for organizing the intricate details of our daily lives. Without bureaucracy, modern society would collapse. It would be impossible to run any of the large public and private organizations we depend on without bureaucracy's division of labor and hierarchy of authority. The challenge is to keep these necessary structures of our civilization flexible, efficient, and capable of innovation.

More than 200 years after the drafting of the Constitution, Americans still rely on government but also mistrust it. These attitudes continue to serve us well. What we mistrust, we are more likely to monitor. And government needs our constant attention if it is to avoid inefficiency, incompetence, and arbitrariness. Without our informed participation, it cannot serve us individually or help us as a people to attain the lofty goals of the Founding Fathers.

On December 11, 1998, the day before the Judiciary Committee's vote authorizing an impeachment inquiry, President Clinton prepares to offer his apology for misleading the country.

CHAPTER 1

The Road to Impeachment

ON AUGUST 17, 1998, President William Jefferson Clinton sat before a television camera to speak to viewers in the United States of America and around the world. His hands, often seen tilted upright in prayer, or shaking the hands of well-wishers, or holding the hands of his wife and teenage daughter, were now pressed together, pointing downward, on his lap.

". . . I misled people. Including even my wife," the president admitted to his supporters and enemies. "I deeply regret that."

President Clinton explained that he had held back the truth because prosecutors began investigating his private life, when they could prove no wrongdoing in his business dealings.

Soon, a report of the four-year investigation would show whether the House of Representatives had enough evidence to impeach President Clinton. A presidential **impeachment** meant that the House would formally accuse Clinton of "treason, bribery, or other high

James McDougal, one of President Clinton's partners in the Whitewater real estate investment scrutinized during a four-year investigation by the House of Representatives, speaks to the press.

crimes and **misdemeanors.**" These crimes were specified in Article II, Section 4 of the United States Constitution.

Tangled Yarns of Suspicion

In the 1980s, Bill Clinton, then governor of Arkansas, and his wife, Hillary Rodham Clinton, invested money in land, or "real estate." Whitewater, one of the housing developments planned for this real estate, would indeed prove rough waters for the future First Family.

The Clintons' partners in this deal included James Mc-Dougal. His bank, Madison Guaranty Savings and Loan, was supposed to be paying for much of the land development. However, Madison Guaranty kept lending money to people who would not or could not repay the bank. When those people defaulted on their loans, the U.S. government had to pay the bank back.

In effect, McDougal was giving away bank money—about $60 million—that belonged to other people. To make matters worse, many of the housing developments were never completed. That meant that investors could not earn back their money. The government shut down the bank for this fraudulent behavior, and many people, including the Clintons, lost tens of thousands of dollars.

In August 1994, U.S. Attorney General Janet Reno replaced special prosecutor Robert Fiske with an independent counsel, Kenneth Starr. (By coincidence, the law allowing independent counsels was made after impeachment proceedings concerning President Richard Nixon took place. See Chapter 4.) Reno asked Starr to continue investigating whether the Clintons had a role in Madison Guaranty's fraud.

In 1996 a judge convicted James McDougal on 18 felony counts relating to the loans he made through Madison Guaranty. Other partners were convicted, too, of crimes including loan fraud and obstruction (blocking) of justice.

But prosecutors never proved that the Clintons committed crimes as investors. Prosecutors also investigated the Rose Law Firm, where Hillary Clinton—a lawyer like her husband—handled some of Madison Guaranty's legal work. They could not find any evidence that Hillary Clinton committed crimes through her business either.

Fiske's investigation of the Rose Firm did, however, find more tangles. Hillary Clinton's law firm partners included Vincent Foster and Webster Hubbell. They both handled Whitewater legal issues, too. When Bill Clinton won the presidency in 1992, Foster and Hubbell came to Washington, D.C., to work in Clinton's new administration. Foster became deputy White House counsel, and Hubbell became associate attorney general at the Department of Justice.

Foster worked on public matters, but he also continued to handle the Clintons' personal tax and legal matters—including Whitewater. When Foster committed suicide in July 1993, some of the Clintons' paperwork disappeared from Foster's office. Naturally, suspicions grew.

Shortly thereafter, Fiske turned up evidence that Hubbell had stolen nearly $500,000 from the Rose Law Firm. Hubbell's crime, to which he pleaded guilty, earned him fines, prison time, and disbarment. He could no longer practice law.

The Starr Report

In England in 1701, Edward, Earl of Oxford, was impeached for hiring someone "known to be a person of ill fame and reputation." In late 20th-century America, however, President Clinton faced little punishment for being friends with convicted felons, as long as he committed no crimes himself.

In England in 1666, impeachment was sought against Viscount John Mordaunt for making "uncivil addresses to a woman." In the late 20th century, however, American voters did not seem to care about Clinton's "addresses" to many women. Suspecting that he might have been unfaithful to his wife, voters still elected Clinton president in 1992 and reelected him in 1996.

Rumors of Clinton's affairs with even more women led Kenneth Starr to test that 330-year-old English **precedent.** Just before his appointment as independent counsel, Starr encouraged and helped lawyers for Paula Jones to pursue a civil lawsuit against Clinton.

The United States Supreme Court ruled in May 1996 that Paula Jones could indeed sue President Clinton while he was in office for something he did before he became president. Jones accused Clinton of sexual harassment because he allegedly tried to have sexual contact with her when he was Arkansas governor in 1991.

During the Jones trial, lawyers tried to prove that President Clinton had a history of sexual harassment by asking several women to testify about his behavior. Monica Lewinsky, a young unpaid White House worker or "intern," confided to a friend that she had had sexual relations with President Clinton in the White House.

In January 1998, Clinton denied under oath that he had sexual relations with the intern. With his wife by his side, he told a television audience, "I did not have sexual

Former White House intern Monica Lewinsky speaks publicly about her sexual relationship with President Clinton.

relations with that woman, Miss Lewinsky." The Jones trial proceeded. That April, however, a judge ruled that Paula Jones had not proven harassment. The judge threw out the lawsuit.

Although Clinton may have won that battle, he still faced a war. Starr had stockpiled the following evidence as ammunition: Lewinsky's audiotaped details about her affair with the president, logbook entries of her Oval Office visits, and an exhibit of gifts exchanged between Clinton and Lewinsky. Starr **subpoenaed** President Clinton to testify to a grand jury about his relationship and whether he had asked Lewinsky to lie in the Jones case.

Only after President Clinton testified on August 17, 1998, did he admit to the country, "Indeed, I did have a relationship with Miss Lewinsky that was not appropriate. In fact it was wrong."

Members of Congress who had supported the president throughout all the investigations felt betrayed. Jim Moran, a **Democratic** representative from Virginia, resented the fact that he had to explain the situation to his children. He likened the scandal to a novel full of "bizarre, sleazy characters. . . . I guess there are no real heroes."

Dianne Feinstein, Democratic senator from California, stated, "My trust in [the president's] credibility has been badly shattered."

Democrat Tom Daschle, the Senate minority leader from South Dakota, said, "I'm disappointed in not being told the truth. . . . [But] it's time we get on with it."

Members of the House Judiciary Committee, meeting on October 5, 1998, recommend that Congress open a formal investigation on the grounds for impeachment.

"Get on" with what? Impeachment? Had Starr won the war?

On September 9, the independent counsel released a 445-page report, which displayed Starr's evidence of impeachable offenses. Congress received copies of the Starr Report and decided to make the report public. After all, it had been funded by $40 million of the taxpayers' money. Newspapers published the report, and it was posted on the Internet for anyone in the world to read.

The war raged: on one side, the **Republicans** who controlled the majority in the House of Representatives and the Senate; on the other side, the Democrats, the political party of the president.

- On October 5, by a vote of 21 Republicans to 16 Democrats, the House Judiciary Committee recommended that Congress open a formal investigation of the grounds for impeaching President Clinton.
- On October 8, the House of Representatives voted along party lines again to authorize an impeachment inquiry.
- On December 12, again following party lines, the Judiciary Committee approved four articles of impeachment. Its report said:

William Jefferson Clinton has undermined the integrity of his office, has brought disrepute on the Presidency, has betrayed his trust as President, and has acted in a manner subversive of the rule of law and justice, to the manifest injury of the people of the United States.

Wherefore, William Jefferson Clinton, by such conduct, warrants impeachment and trial, and removal from office and disqualification to hold and enjoy any office of honor, trust or profit under the United States.

Article I, perjury, charged that, under oath, Clinton lied to and misled the grand jury on August 17, 1998, about one or more subjects.

Article II, perjury, charged that Clinton, under oath, lied on two occasions on January 17, 1998, during the Paula Jones case.

Article III, obstruction of justice, charged that Clinton acted seven separate times to block the due course of justice. For example, the article charged that he asked his secretary to hide gifts he'd given to Lewinsky and that he asked Lewinsky to lie about their relationship.

Article IV, abuse of power, charged that Clinton lied and/or evaded answers to 81 questions the Judiciary Committee posed to him in a letter.

In the weeks between the Judiciary Committee's first report and the full House of Representatives impeachment vote, the world's other business continued. U.S. and British planes bombed Iraq for preventing the United Nations from inspecting factories that could make biological and chemical weapons. (These inspections were a condition of a treaty ending the Gulf War.) Serbia continued attacking ethnic Albanians in the Kosovo province. In the United States, soaring stock prices set new market records and unemployment achieved new lows.

Holiday shoppers gave President Clinton his highest on-the-job ratings. In a *Time* magazine poll, 68 percent of Americans said they did not want the president impeached. Unlike attitudes toward Presidents Andrew Johnson and Richard Nixon, who had also faced impeachment controversies, many Americans identified with the man who rose from near-poverty in Hope, Arkansas. To show their support in the November elections, voters replaced five Republican representatives with five Democrats—the president's political party.

Some Republicans suggested dropping the whole impeachment hot potato, so they wouldn't be blamed for impeaching a popular president. The Senate majority leader, Republican Trent Lott, was said by *Time* magazine to be "more allergic to impeachment than Clinton was." Lott

Stock prices reached record highs on the floor of the New York Stock Exchange in February 1998. This distracted Americans from the impeachment investigation and contributed to President Clinton receiving his highest on-the-job ratings.

feared that a Senate trial would bog down other important issues the Republicans wanted to nurture into legislation.

On Saturday, December 19, however, the House of Representatives did vote to impeach Clinton. The 42nd president of the United States was only the second president in history to be impeached. Representatives voted 228 to 206 to approve Article I; 229 to 205 to reject Article II; 221 to 212 to approve Article III; and 285 to 148 to reject Article IV. Following the vote, the American public gave President Clinton his highest job-approval rating—75 percent.

The Senate's first order of business in 1999, the last year of the millennium: putting President Bill Clinton on trial for perjury and obstruction of justice.

Leaders of the 13 states, after
winning freedom from England
in 1776, wanted to be governed
by a stronger set of common
laws. They elected George
Washington to lead the 1787
Constitutional Convention in
Philadelphia for this purpose.

CHAPTER 2

Impeachment: A Constitutional View

WHY DOES OUR COUNTRY have such a measure as impeachment? When a professional baseball team doesn't win many games, the team owner fires the manager. When a company feels that an employee is not doing a good job anymore, the boss fires that employee. When a police officer is suspected of doing something wrong, the police chief can suspend the officer, with or without pay, until an investigation proves or disproves guilt.

So, what happens when our elected representatives believe a president has done wrong? Our representatives try to impeach the president.

Many people believe that to impeach a person means to remove that person from office. That, however, is not true. The word's roots dig down to the Middle English word *empechen* and the Old French word *empechier,* meaning "to hold back" or "to prevent." Today, to impeach someone means "to challenge, discredit, or accuse" a person. The accusation resembles an indictment by a grand jury. Just as a guilty verdict in common-law courts can result in a fine and/or a jail term, so too does a guilty verdict at an impeachment trial have the power to remove an impeached person from office.

Let's look at how our Founding Fathers created this procedure. After the 13 colonies won freedom from England in 1776, they became states and created their own laws. A weak set of laws, called the Articles of Confederation, linked the states. However, the states ran into trouble when they tried to trade with each other or with other countries. Trying to extend their borders, some states overlapped land claimed by other states. For example, New York declared that it owned the land claimed by Vermont. Virginia claimed it owned Kentucky, and North Carolina claimed Tennessee.

Leaders of the states agreed to create a stronger set of common laws, or a constitution, that would govern all people no matter which state they lived in. Representatives from five states gathered first in Annapolis, Maryland, to make changes in the Articles of Confederation. They agreed to meet again at the Constitutional Convention of 1787 to debate the changes. These state representatives became known as the framers of the Constitution. And their first deed was to elect George Washington as the leader of the convention.

An important idea shaping the Constitution was the system of checks and balances to enforce separations of power. This system would ensure that none of the three branches of government would ever become stronger than, or act like a bully over, the others. The legislative branch (Congress, consists of the House of Representatives and the Senate) would create the laws; the executive branch (the president) would approve or veto (reject) the laws; and the judicial branch (the courts) would interpret and enforce the laws.

An example of checks and balances outside of government is the structure of professional sports. Player unions

A manuscript draft of the United States Constitution (left) and the only known copy of its first printing (right).

I.

II.

and owner associations can propose and vote on rules. Once passed, these rules are interpreted and enforced by referees and umpires. These officials can sometimes overrule each other, in the same way that judges can overturn decisions made in lower courts.

An important check our framers borrowed from the English Parliament was the ability to remove someone from power. They believed that fear of being kicked out of office would prevent officials from doing wrong. This belief was so strong, in fact, that between 1776 and 1787, several states, including New Jersey, North Carolina, Vermont, and Pennsylvania, had already created and enforced their own impeachment laws for governors, judges, and representatives.

The houses of Parliament in London, England. Impeachment processes originated in the House of Commons and were tried by the House of Lords.

So when the framers of the Constitution met in Philadelphia, they had to cobble together pieces of impeachment law from different states with changes they wanted in the English law. The debates began.

The framers had to decide:

1. Who could be impeached;
2. What the punishment would be;
3. How impeachment would work;
4. For what reasons someone could be impeached.

Who Can Be Impeached?

Working from the Virginia Plan—which served as a draft of the Constitution—and other state impeachment laws, the framers agreed that executive officials such as presidents, vice presidents, and governors could be impeached. And Article I, Section 5 stated that Congress, with a two-thirds majority, could expel one of its own members.

However, during these debates, the framers noted that Supreme Court judges hold their offices for life. They are appointed by the president and confirmed by Congress. Citizens could not show their displeasure of the judges' work by voting them in and out of office—as they could do with presidents and members of Congress. The framers agreed to include judges in the wording of the law. Therefore, Article II, Section 4 of the Constitution begins:

> The President, Vice President and all civil officers of the United States . . .

What Will the Punishment Be?

In England during colonial times, impeached and convicted officers could be fined, removed from office, imprisoned, or put to death—any or all of the above! Our Constitution's framers considered punishment by death too harsh. In fact, most of the state versions of impeachment law had already deleted the punishment of bodily harm. In Article I, which assigns powers to the legislature, Section 3 states:

> Judgment in cases of impeachment shall not extend further than to removal from Office, and disqualification to hold and enjoy any Office of honor, Trust or Profit under the United States. . . .

The section goes on to state that impeached persons can still face civil or criminal trial in the public sector for crimes they committed in office.

Therefore, Article II, Section 4 on impeachment specifies:

> The President, Vice President and all civil officers of the United States, shall be removed from office . . .

How Does Impeachment Work?

In colonial Virginia, regular courts handled impeachments. Therefore, at the Constitutional Convention, Virginia's Edmund Randolph proposed that a national judiciary try impeachments. New York delegate Alexander Hamilton agreed, as did James Madison. However, other states had impeachment processes begin in the lower legislative houses or in a council. Then the upper house conducted the trial. This procedure mirrored England's system of impeachment by the House of Commons and trial by the House of Lords.

After a long summer of tense debate, a detail committee won acceptance for this clause: "The Senate of the United States shall have the power to try all impeachments; but no person shall be convicted without the concurrence of two-thirds of the members present." Hamilton, not present at the vote, eventually agreed with the language. Madison voted against it.

As for the impeachment trial itself, framers decided it would follow common-law trials. "Managers" from the House of Representatives would act as prosecutors and present evidence and testimony. The Senate would act as an impartial jury. The chief justice of the Supreme Court would preside over the trial.

Therefore, Article II, Section 4 continues:

> The President, Vice President and all civil officers of the United States, shall be removed from office on impeachment for, and conviction of . . . .

For What Reasons Can Someone Be Impeached?

The grounds for impeachment caused the most controversial debates at the convention. And the grounds have continued to stir up trouble over the past 200 years. In 1970 Republican Representative Gerald Ford (who became the 38th president in 1974) said, ". . . an impeachable offense is whatever a majority of the House of Representatives considers it to be at a given moment in history."

At first, the only grounds for impeachment that the framers considered were corruption, neglect of duty, and misconduct during office. Elected officials already could be removed if convicted of common-law crimes such as murder. A detail committee working on impeachment had already specified the crimes of **treason** and **bribery.**

The framers, though, wanted the list of impeachable offenses to reach beyond regular crimes. Their precedent was a seven-year impeachment process going on in England. William Hastings, governor general of India (then a colony of England), was impeached for bad policies—not for crimes such as treason. He was later acquitted by the House of Lords. Impeachment essentially vanished in England after his trial. Citing the Hastings impeachment, George Mason of Virginia also wanted bad governing included. He suggested adding the word "maladministration." However, the framers felt that *anybody* could use this vague word if he or she disagreed with how someone did his or her job. Mason then proposed "high crimes and misdemeanors," and the language passed the vote.

So the Constitution's Article II, Section 4 stood as:

> The President, Vice President and all civil officers of the United States, shall be removed from office on impeachment for, and conviction of, treason, bribery, or other high crimes and misdemeanors.

The Constitution is a living, working document. By design, its laws can be amended and interpreted in many ways. This design allows the Constitution to grow and adapt to the changing needs of America's citizens. But this very flexibility causes citizens to disagree about how to apply laws. Since 1787, lawyers have debated what exactly "high crimes and misdemeanors" are. Later, you will see how this catchall term ensnared some officials and missed trapping others.

Colonial Williamsburg, Virginia, where the colony's General Assembly met in 1635 to demand the removal of the royal governor of Virginia. They believed he had harmed the colony's business interests.

CHAPTER **3**

Nonpresidential Impeachment

Impeachment, Pre-Constitution Style

AS EARLY AS 1635, colonists had begun to use impeachment powers to test their independence. They tried to oust officials who had been appointed by England's rulers and Parliament.

For example, in 1635 the royal governor of Virginia, John Harvey, was angering the councillors (representatives of the colony's counties). United as a General Assembly, the councillors charged that Harvey kept tobacco planters from renegotiating contracts with England. The councillors also accused Harvey of pitting Maryland's traders against Virginia's and signing a dangerous treaty with American Indians.

The General Assembly demanded Harvey's removal from office. It sent him back to England for trial. However, Parliament members had no interest in impeaching Harvey—someone they themselves had appointed. In fact, they returned him to office! Despite this slap in the face, the colonists began to feel that they could challenge British law. Their nerve and their power grew.

Those Virginia colonists had used the term "petition of grievances" to describe their impeachment action against Harvey. (Harvey's friends called it a mutiny.) It wasn't until 1657 that colonists recorded the use of the word impeachment. Roger Williams, president of Providence Plantations, asked Rhode Island's General Court to arrest a citizen, William Harris, and to bring "an impeachment of high treason." For evidence, Williams sent Harris's writings to court. But because Williams never appeared in court to accuse Harris face to face, the charges never made it to trial. Rhode Island, a chartered colony, was not under direct English rule. Williams did, however, borrow the English legal maneuver of impeachment.

More colonists began to take matters into their own hands. Instead of hoping for justice in England, they began putting impeached officials on trial in the colonies. Such a trial in Maryland in 1669 stressed the importance of following legal procedure. Lawyer John Morecroft, a member of Maryland's assembly, faced trial for misconduct, yet Maryland's charter had no rules for impeachment. Morecroft pointed out to the court the unfairness of his trial. The court acquitted him, instructing the assembly to follow parliamentary process in the future.

Rugged life in the colonies, however, did not lend itself to proper English law. How should one deal with an official who murdered Native Americans in peacetime? If remote settlements had no court, who would rule in a trial? Could impeached persons appeal their decisions? To whom?

The colonies' different grounds and procedures for impeachment produced a wild variety of precedents. Partly because of the confused state of impeachment law, all impeachment efforts failed between 1700 and 1750. This confusion showed why the states needed to unite under a stronger constitution.

Rugged life in the colonies did not lend itself to proper English law. Here Pilgrims war with Indians in 17th century Massachusetts.

In the second half of the 18th century, the French and Indian War (1754–1763) caused an increasing number of colonists to resent British power. Impeachment became less a tool to punish *individuals* appointed by the English and more a legal means to question English *law*. In other words, impeachment grew as a way for legislators— elected by the colonists themselves—to *check* the ultimate executive branch, the king of England.

Impeachment cases in Pennsylvania, South Carolina, and Massachusetts accused officials of breaking laws established by the colonies—not by England. None other than Benjamin Franklin in Philadelphia and John Adams in Boston participated on the side of the colonies. The Pennsylvania and South Carolina impeachments failed; the successful Massachusetts impeachment did not reach trial. However, precedents from these proceedings helped guide the Constitution's framers in 1787. These efforts emphasized the commoners' check on their leaders.

Key Federal Cases, 1787 to the Present

Pre-Constitution impeachment proceedings focused more on law than on politics. However, after the Constitution gave birth to the federal government, national politics began to plague impeachment cases.

U.S. Senator William Blount

On July 5, 1797, William Blount, a senator from Tennessee, was accused of high crimes and misdemeanors. He became the first U.S. senator to face impeachment charges.

Blount had been caught trying to get Cherokee and Creek Indians to join England in an invasion of Florida. The territory belonged to Spain at that time. The House approved five **articles of impeachment.** They ranged from attempting to seduce a government employee into joining the plot to the very serious charge of violating the Spanish-American Boundary Treaty of 1795.

Blount's guilt was never in doubt; he had even confessed. But the impeachment raised some questions concerning the very senators and representatives who were accusing Blount:

1. Because the Senate had actually expelled Blount that July, should Blount be tried as a senator?
2. Since Blount was now a private citizen, could any private citizen be impeached?
3. Does the language in Article II, Section 4, "all civil officers of the United States," mean that senators are civil officers who can be impeached too?

Faced with trying one of its own, the Senate was acting nothing like an impartial jury. The two main political parties—the Federalists and the Republicans—argued over whether a senator could be impeached at all. In theory most senators on both sides did not want impeachment to cover themselves.

One Federalist senator, Jacob Read of South Carolina, proposed a motion. It equated senators with ordinary citizens, who could not be impeached. This idea was another way colonists wanted their impeachment law to differ from England's. In England, under universal liability, all citizens—including lords—could be impeached. Republicans, however, argued that ordinary citizens who committed, say, treason, should be impeached. They should be prevented from ever holding office.

In the end the Senate refused to try Blount as either a senator or a private citizen. Blount had already been punished by expulsion, a measure the Constitution granted to members of Congress. Impeaching him as a private citizen would be like giving a student detention after he or she was already expelled from the school. More to the point, senators felt that impeaching citizens would violate the separation of power between the federal government and the states. If citizens could not be impeached, then Congress members could not be impeached either.

Judge John Pickering, Circuit Court, New Hampshire

Unlike presidents, members of Congress, and elected state officials, judges are appointed for life. However, these appointments are political. The people who happen to be in power appoint judges who believe in the same political principles.

But what happens when new people come into power? That's exactly what President John Adams (a **Federalist**) was worried about when Thomas Jefferson (a Democratic-Republican) was elected president in 1801. One of Adams's last measures was appointing new justices of the peace and federal judges to fill a new circuit court system. These appointees became known as "the midnight judges," because they were proposed, confirmed, and commissioned all in one day.

As a result, one of Jefferson's first measures was to see how many of those judges he could *unappoint.* He repealed Adams's judiciary act and set about ousting other judges.

The Pickering case debated the grounds for impeachment. Judge Pickering was slipping into alcoholic insanity, swearing and hollering from the bench. (The medical community had not yet identified alcoholism as a disease in 1801.) Did alcoholism, however, constitute a high crime or misdemeanor? A larger question loomed: If the new administration could impeach for alcoholism, what else could be considered grounds for impeachment?

The tricky part of this trial was that almost everyone agreed Pickering had to go. He was simply unfit to rule in court. The Senate trial did find Pickering guilty, and he was removed from the bench. However, the senators worded their ruling in such a way as to show that Pickering did not commit a high crime or misdemeanor. In sidestepping the issue as it did in Blount's case, the Senate accomplished the task of removing the accused from office. Scholars still argue over whether the Senate's action was constitutional.

Supreme Court Justice Samuel Chase

From the end of the 18th century through the beginning of the 19th century, the Federalists and the Republicans continued to battle, using impeachment as their sword.

In 1804 Justice Samuel Chase, a republican during the Revolution, was now openly using his court to promote Federalist ideals. For example, Chase thought freedom of the press would harm the government. Over the course of several cases he heard as a justice, Chase gave biased instructions to jurors to sway their opinions, refused to let lawyers (with Republican ideals) perform their normal court duties, and denied citizens (again, those with Republican ideals) their civil rights and liberties. President Jefferson pressured the House of Representatives to impeach Chase.

The constitutional question this case raised was whether someone could be impeached for promoting his beliefs—a deed that is not necessarily a crime, not even a

Supreme Court Justice Samuel Chase faced impeachment for promoting his Federalist beliefs that the central government and the states should share power. He was acquitted by the Senate in 1804.

misdemeanor—in common law. The question echoed Pickering's dilemma, this time at the federal level.

Chase's lawyers argued that Chase had not committed his actions dishonestly. He sincerely believed his actions were protecting the new nation. The Senate acquitted Chase on all eight articles of impeachment.

Scholar Irving Brant concluded, "justices of the Supreme Court could be removed from office only for 'high crimes and misdemeanors' which were either serious indictable offenses or willful violations of their oath of office."

No judge could be removed for merely having beliefs or ideals opposite those of the people in power—the president or the majority in Congress.

Supreme Court Justice William O. Douglas, 1969–1970

Supreme Court Justice William Douglas faced impeachment threats for exercising his ideals in the same way

Samuel Chase had. However, while Chase had wanted to repress negative opinions about the government, Douglas believed free speech and a free press helped keep a government strong and responsible to its people. Douglas also devoted himself to improving civil rights for African Americans—still a controversial cause in the 1960s.

In this case, impeachment was actually used as a tool to prove Douglas's *innocence.* On the floor of the House, many representatives were speaking out against Douglas. To begin with, they were angry that the Senate had rejected two of Republican President Nixon's appointees to the Supreme Court. The representatives resented Douglas's devotion to civil rights and his liberal views. They also charged that Douglas had a "conflict of interest," because he was consulting for a Democratic organization at the same time that he was serving on the Supreme Court. They felt this work influenced his judicial decisions.

Gerald Ford, then Republican minority leader, asked that a special committee be formed to investigate Douglas. Such a request would have to be referred to the House Rules Committee, headed by a man who believed in segregating blacks from whites.

Knowing that such an investigation could take years (as in Starr's investigation of Clinton), Douglas's supporters decided to use impeachment as a new strategy. A request for impeachment would have to be referred to the House Committee on the Judiciary, a more impartial committee, then led by a Douglas supporter.

Representative Andrew Jacobs Jr., a Republican from Indiana, interrupted Ford's speech. He challenged and convinced Ford to introduce a resolution to impeach Douglas. The trick worked. Five months later, a judiciary subcommittee produced a 924-page report finding no grounds for impeachment. Douglas was cleared.

Spiro T. Agnew, 1973, the Impeachment That Never Was

Shortly after the inquiry into William Douglas, Vice President Spiro Agnew tried to get the House of Representatives to begin an impeachment inquiry on himself! Agnew felt that news reporters, fed by unidentified reliable sources in the Justice Department, were accus-

Vice President Spiro T. Agnew at an August 1973 news conference during which he stated he would not resign.

ing him of accepting bribes from contractors when he had been governor of Maryland. Because these allegations came during investigations of the Watergate scandal (see Chapter 4), the public's opinion of the government was plummeting.

Agnew's lawyers argued that a regular court could not indict him for bribery unless the House impeached him first. They claimed that a thorough legal proceeding such as an impeachment might even clear Agnew's reputation.

To support his petition for impeachment, Agnew used a precedent established in 1826 by Vice President John Calhoun. Calhoun had faced bribery charges of accepting $15,000 when he was secretary of war. The House began an investigation and cleared Calhoun's name when the results proved no wrongdoing.

Unfortunately for Agnew, the Justice Department presented plenty of evidence of his crimes. Agnew resigned as vice president, paid a fine, and served no jail time. Gerald Ford, who had been the primary force behind Douglas's inquiry, rose from House Speaker to vice president after Agnew's resignation. As you will see in Chapter 4, Ford's ascent to power had not yet ended.

Presidents Andrew Johnson and Richard M. Nixon occupied the White House during times when the American people were deeply divided by war.

CHAPTER **4**

Two Presidents Face the Fire

Andrew Johnson, "Accidental President"

FOLLOWING THE ASSASSINATION OF President Abraham Lincoln in April 1865, Vice President Andrew Johnson stepped into the presidency. Stepping into a lion's den might have been easier. The Civil War—the cause of 600,000 deaths—had just ended, but the fighting in Congress still raged.

During the Reconstruction period, Congress and the whole country debated several issues:

1. Should the Confederate states (the 11 Southern states that fought to separate from the United States) be welcomed back into the Union as if they had never left?

President Johnson, a former Tennessee senator who didn't want to separate from the Union, and the late President Lincoln believed the

Confederate states should resume their places in Congress. How could Congress pass national laws without them?

2. Or, must the Confederate states earn back their representation by agreeing to certain conditions? Lincoln and Johnson believed that individual rebel leaders and plantation owners had to be punished. But most members of Congress believed the rebel state *governments* needed to be punished.

3. Should the freed slaves receive the rights to vote and own property? Postwar Congress, led by the Radical Republicans, believed the slaves should. Johnson, despite Lincoln's issuing of the Emancipation Proclamation in 1863, believed that the four million freed slaves should not become full citizens.

Johnson had owned slaves before the war and had publicly remarked that whites were superior to blacks. He suggested that the states should develop their own voting rules and that blacks could apply to their states for the right to vote. In 1865 the governments of Connecticut, Wisconsin, and Minnesota actually defeated proposals for the black vote. Michigan, Ohio, and Kansas did the same. In theory many white people wanted the slaves to be freed; in reality, many whites didn't want the slaves to become equal in society and politics. After all, hadn't the Constitution stated that slaves counted as only three-fifths of a person?

The Radical Republicans decided to amend the Constitution. As part of the Reconstruction Acts, Congress passed three important amendments: The 13th Amendment (1865) prohibits slavery. The 14th Amendment (1868) forbids states from passing laws that take away a person's life, liberty, or property without "due process of law," (i.e., a trial by a jury of peers). It also guarantees that all people have equal protection under our legal system. The 15th Amendment (1870) states that federal or state governments cannot prevent people from voting because of race or color.

Johnson vetoed—legally disapproved—these amendments. (He had also voted against earlier bills granting rights to blacks.) The majority in Congress, however, overruled Johnson's veto. These three amendments became part of our Constitution. In fact, a hundred years later Supreme Court Justice Douglas was still fighting to make sure the descendants of the freed slaves received these basic rights.

While these legislative vetoes and overrules are part of our government's system of checks and balances, many congressmen wanted a stronger check against Johnson and his policies. Before its successful impeachment of Johnson, Congress actually tried to impeach him two other times. His enemies in Congress came up with creative ways to show their hatred of Johnson. Johnson was "an aching tooth in the national jaw, a screeching infant in a crowded lecture room." Another called him an "ungrateful, despicable, besotted traitorous man."

Johnson's downfall gathered speed with his policy of dividing the Confederate states into districts run by Union soldiers. His own secretary of war, Edwin Stanton, did not approve of this measure.

Upon hearing rumors that Johnson might fire Stanton, Congress passed the "Tenure of Office" Act. This act forbade the president from removing a department head without Senate approval. Naturally, Johnson vetoed this act. The Constitution stated that the president had the right— the responsibility, even—to appoint *and* remove people from certain offices. But Congress again overruled Johnson and passed the act.

About a year later, in February 1868, Johnson finally removed Stanton. In a hasty three days, the House of Representatives voted 126 to 47 to impeach Johnson on 11 articles—10 having to do with Stanton's removal. The weak 11th article accused Johnson of threatening Congress. Johnson's secretary of the navy, Gideon Welles, said the Republicans would have impeached Johnson "had he been accused of stepping on a dog's tail."

The Senate trial began in March. After two months of testimony and evidence, the Senate voted along party lines on all the articles: 35, guilty; 19, not guilty. However, each article tally lacked one vote to achieve a two-thirds majority to convict Johnson.

All of the seven Republicans who crossed the party line to vote not guilty lost their seats in the next election. The one deciding vote, cast by Kansas Republican Senator Edmund Ross, turned Ross into a friendless pauper. A telegraph proclaimed, "Kansas repudiates you as she does all perjurers and skunks." However, Democrat John F. Kennedy, who would defeat Richard Nixon for the presidency 100 years later, praised Ross in his book *Profiles in Courage.* Kennedy wrote that Ross rose above politics and "may well have preserved for ourselves and posterity constitutional government in the United States."

Johnson's impeachment raised important legal issues. His defense lawyers argued that the impeachment was actually a "bill of attainder," which the Constitution forbade. Attorney William M. Evarts asked the Senate, "What is a bill of attainder; what is a bill of pains and penalties? . . . It is a proceeding by the legislature . . . to enact crime, sentence, [and] punishment all in one . . . ."

Defense lawyers also argued that Congress impeached Johnson for breaking an *ex post facto* law—committing an act that was not a crime *at the time* it was committed. They rightly claimed that the Tenure of Office Act was unconstitutional. Echoing the trial of Samuel Chase, they said Johnson's behavior resulted from "honest motives" and was not criminal. And Johnson's so-called threatening words—actually very mild ones—against Congress were allowed under the First Amendment's guarantee of freedom of speech.

Johnson, America's first impeached president, remained in office for the few months left in his term. Mobs showed up to jeer him, and his trial attracted thousands of

onlookers. In the end Johnson's policies failed. Instead, the words of Johnson's foe, House Manager Thaddeus Stevens, prevailed. The United States became not "a nest of shrinking cowardly slaves," but "filled with a free, untrammeled people."

Richard Nixon and Dirty Tricks

The free, untrammeled people may not technically have impeached President Richard M. Nixon, but they still accomplished their goal of removing him from the presidency. The people exercised their freedom of speech through a modern political tool called television.

Nixon took office in January 1969 at the height of America's involvement in the Vietnam War. He also assumed power when technology was allowing instant print and television news of the war to reach every home. Watching footage of bomb-wrecked villages and hearing tallies of dead bodies, the American people became bitterly divided. Many Americans did not think that our government

Congress impeached President Andrew Johnson in 1868. Although the constitutionality of the process is still debated, most Americans wanted Johnson out of office.

An estimated 100,000 Vietnam protesters from all over the United States and Canada assembled in Washington, D.C., on November 4, 1967, for a mass anti-war rally.

should sacrifice our soldiers in another country's civil war, fought halfway around the world. Others thought that America had a responsibility to stop the spread of Communism throughout the world. (Communism is an economic and political theory under which all people share the country's wealth. In practice, Communism often smothers individuals' rights, and results in the government's control of politics, business, education, media, sports, etc.)

Americans took to the streets to protest in greater numbers for more reasons than ever before. African Americans were continuing their quest for civil rights. Increasing numbers of women were asserting their claim for equal rights—for example, equal pay and opportunity for the same jobs that men had. The U.S. government now had to share the media coverage with the common people's protests and demands.

Only five months after Nixon was inaugurated as president, he committed the first of his many illegal acts. He ordered *wiretaps* installed in the offices and homes of newspaper reporters and White House aides. (A wiretap is a small device that allows people to listen in on and record the activities of other people. Police can only use this measure if a judge approves it.) Nixon felt these people disagreed with his Vietnam War policies, especially the bombing of Cambodia, a country next to Vietnam. Soon members of Congress discovered that they were being wiretapped, or spied on, too. One member of Congress, House Majority Leader Hale Boggs, spoke out against these wiretaps. A year later, Boggs mysteriously disappeared during a flight over Alaska.

In June 1972—five months before the next presidential election—aides of Richard Nixon burglarized offices in the Watergate Hotel in Washington, D.C. The offices belonged to the Democratic National Committee, which would soon nominate a candidate to face Nixon in the election. The aides were caught and convicted. Their activity was not only illegal, it was also foolish and unnecessary. Nixon defeated Democrat George McGovern by a landslide in the 1972 election.

Congress formed committees to investigate whether Nixon ordered the burglary and wiretappings and whether he tried to cover up his actions once the burglars had been caught. These committees worked for more than a year, gathering and reviewing evidence, reading transcripts of the burglars' trials, and finally interviewing witnesses. Citizens could watch some of these proceedings on television. Many people felt that Congress was dragging its feet on investigating Nixon, and the people began to clamor for impeachment.

For a change, Congress was not divided over impeachment, with Democrats on one side and Republicans (Nixon's party) on the other. Republicans—especially those facing elections in November 1974—did not want to appear as if they were siding with a criminal.

In June 1972, aides of Richard Nixon burglarized the offices of the Democratic National Committee in the Watergate Hotel in Washington, D.C.

Although Democrats wanted Nixon impeached, they didn't mind if the process dragged on. They could use the scandal to embarrass Republicans in the upcoming election.

Ironically, Nixon's tape-recording of his enemies backfired. The Judiciary Committee subpoenaed tapes of all the conversations Nixon had made in *his* office. In July 1974, a misplaced White House tape surfaced. On it Nixon was heard asking an aide to work with the Central Intelligence Agency (CIA) to prevent the investigation of the Watergate burglaries.

With evidence of bribery, fraud, and conspiracy, the House Judiciary Committee adopted three articles of impeachment: obstruction of justice, abuse of power, and noncompliance with subpoenas. Coincidentally, Hillary Rodham, who would soon marry Bill Clinton, worked as a lawyer for this committee. And Republican Representative Henry Hyde from Illinois, who would later help impeach Bill Clinton, supported Nixon.

The House later accepted the committee's report with a bipartisan vote of 412 to 3. But before the House could officially impeach him, Richard Nixon resigned.

President Richard M. Nixon gives his trademark "victory" sign after resigning the presidency on August 9, 1974. Nixon resigned before the House could officially impeach him.

In his resignation speech, he did not mention impeachment. Rather, he admitted in a televised address, "It has become evident to me that I no longer have a strong enough political base in the Congress. . . . Therefore, I shall resign the presidency effective at noon tomorrow."

The country got a new president: Gerald Ford, who had replaced Vice President Agnew less than a year earlier. A month later, to everyone's shock, Ford pardoned Nixon for all his crimes "known and unknown." As a result, Nixon could not even be tried in a criminal court for his misdeeds. Most people's shock over Ford's act did not last long. The people, having achieved their will, were ready to move on. They would be grateful to Nixon for only one thing: finally bringing the soldiers home from Vietnam.

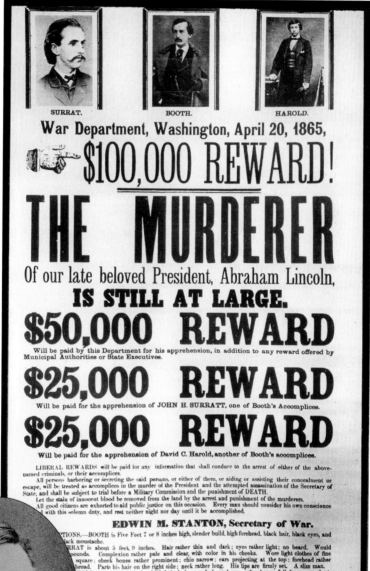

Four U.S. presidents have been removed from office by assassination. Abraham Lincoln (inset) was shot five days after the Civil War ended. A large reward (left) was offered for the apprehension of his assassin.

CHAPTER **5**

Removal By Other Means

PRESIDENTS ANDREW JOHNSON, Richard Nixon, and Bill Clinton would not call impeachment a pleasant experience. Compared to other ways of removing leaders, though, this nonviolent, orderly proceeding let these men off the hook easily.

Outside of holding new elections, the most popular way to remove leaders against their will has been by assassination—murder for political reasons. Assassins claimed the lives of 20 Roman emperors, 31 of Ireland's kings between 4 and 1172 A.D., 9 Japanese premiers since 1860, and 4 U.S. presidents. In recent history, President Ronald Reagan was critically injured by a would-be assassin's bullets.

Most Americans learn about the assassinations of the popular U.S. Presidents Abraham Lincoln and John F. Kennedy in school. Only five days after the Civil War ended, the actor John Wilkes Booth shot Lincoln in Ford's Theater, and proclaimed, "The South is avenged!" Kennedy was gunned down while he rode past the Texas School Book

Depository in Dallas. A man named Lee Harvey Oswald was arrested. Because Oswald also was murdered just two days later, questions about a larger conspiracy still cling like cobwebs to Kennedy's assassination.

Two other presidents were assassinated. On July 2, 1881, James Garfield was shot in a Washington train station. He had been on his way to the New Jersey shore for his vacation. He died of his wounds September 19. President William McKinley was shot on September 6, 1901, and died of his wounds on September 14.

Although the Garfield and McKinley assassins did not kill to advance a political cause, most assassinations are intended to produce political change. Indeed, many of the murders occur during revolutions or spark revolutions. For example, the assassinations of Czar Nicholas II, his family, and appointed officials ended Russia's royal rule in 1917, and cleared the way for the Communists to take over. In Iraq the assassination of Crown Princes Faisal II and Abdul Illah in 1958 capped a military overthrow, or *coup d'état.* It, too, ended royal rule, and the country began a chaotic series of different governments.

Assassinations and revolutions don't always produce the desired political effect right away—or at all. In France the rise of the common people, represented in the government as the Third Estate, led to the toppling of the monarchy in September 1792. France was a republic, declared the new National Convention. The republic beheaded King Louis XVI on January 21, 1793 (and his wife, Marie Antoinette, in October 1793).

The execution of the French king did not end the Revolution. The Jacobin party, led by Maximilien Robespierre, purged its opponents from the government and murdered many of them. The Jacobins succeeded in defending the new republic against Austria, Prussia, England, Holland, and Spain, but they created a reign of terror within France's borders. They clamped down on the freedoms of speech and religion and beheaded those—even supporters—who dared to criticize the new government. In 1794 Robespierre and many Jacobins were led to the guillotine and executed in the manner they had preferred for their enemies. A series of fleeting leaders and violent uprisings followed, until Napoleon Bonaparte proclaimed a new constitution in 1799. France followed its new emperor into an era of expansion.

Sometimes assassination produces the desired political result, but it doesn't last. Austrian Archduke Francis Ferdinand, heir to the thrones of Austria and Hungary, was assassinated in 1914 because he wanted Bosnia to join the Austro-Hungarian empire. His assassin wanted Bosnia to join Serbia. This murder touched off World War I. The treaties after the war did unite Bosnia, Croatia, and Serbia in a new country: Yugoslavia. But as the recent independence wars in Croatia, Bosnia, and Kosovo demonstrated, the people still disagree on how the region should be governed.

Revolutionaries lead French King Louis XVI from the Tuileries in 1792. Six months later, the republic beheaded the king.

A violent end can also come from a peaceful revolution. Mahatma Gandhi, leader of the Indian Congress Party, led his people in years of non-violent protest against British colonial rule. In 1947, when British Viceroy Lord Louis Mountbatten announced that the British would leave India, he credited Gandhi's civil disobedience for the change in foreign policy. (Martin Luther King Jr. adopted Gandhi's peaceful protest methods for the civil rights movement in the 1960s. Sadly, King was also assassinated as his power was cresting in 1968.)

Dr. Martin Luther King Jr. addresses marchers during his "I Have a Dream" speech at the Lincoln Memorial in 1963. Despite his peaceful protest methods, King was assassinated in 1968.

In January 1948 Gandhi began fasting to protest the separation of Pakistan from India. In Gandhi's own home, a man promoting independence for Pakistan gunned down the Hindu spiritual and political leader. More than 50 years later, the conflict between the two countries still rages, with border skirmishes and tests of new nuclear weapons.

Doing the Right Thing: Leaders Making Themselves Obsolete

The 20th century also saw two oppressive regimes come to an end through negotiation, rather than all-out violent revolution. The leaders made themselves obsolete. They sacrificed their own short-term power for the long-term good.

In February 1990 years of both peaceful and violent protest were coming to a head in South Africa. Blacks wanted an end to *apartheid,* a policy denying black people human and civil rights. Furthermore, nations including the United States were strengthening sanctions against South Africa for its apartheid policy. That meant that the countries made it illegal or expensive for businesses to trade with South Africa.

This combustible mixture of internal strife and foreign economic pressure forced the South African government to act. South African President F. W. de Klerk of the National Party (representing white Afrikaners) released Nelson Mandela, a black leader who had been imprisoned since 1964. Mandela, representing the African National Congress (ANC), and de Klerk began negotiating the end to apartheid. After several years of further talks, occasional violent outbreaks, and international counsel, South Africa held elections open to both blacks and whites in April 1994. The ANC received 63.7 percent of the vote, winning 252 seats in the new 400-seat Parliament. On May 10 Nelson Mandela was inaugurated as president. De Klerk lost power, but together with Mandela, he won the Nobel Peace Prize.

Nelson Mandela salutes supporters in 1994, prior to South Africa's first elections open to both blacks and whites. President F. W. de Klerk was defeated, but he later won the Nobel Peace Prize with Mandela.

When Mikhail Gorbachev was unanimously elected general secretary by the Soviet Union Politburo (a legislative body similar to Congress), he faced a troubled homeland. In 1985, in various republics of the Soviet Union, independence movements were gaining force. The government was wasting money and labor trying to keep up with the United States in the arms race (the build-up of military might). Ethnic groups were fighting each other, and government-run businesses and agencies had trouble paying their employees' salaries and producing goods. Food grew scarce, lines grew long, and the people became disgruntled.

Gorbachev tried to reform the Soviet Union and move it from Communism to democracy. With *perestroika,* a restructuring of the economy, and *glasnost,* an openness allowing freedom of religion, travel, and a bit more freedom of the press, Gorbachev set the Soviet Union on its difficult journey to find peace and prosperity inside and outside of its borders.

Some of his measures worked. Countries including Lithuania, the Ukraine, and Estonia gradually reclaimed their independence. Soviet allies under Communist rule, such as Czechoslovakia and Romania, turned to democracy. New political parties formed to challenge the Communist party, and a new Soviet Parliament made Gorbachev its president. In foreign policy, the Soviet Union made new treaties to increase trade and to limit nuclear weapons. Gorbachev won the Nobel Peace Prize in 1990 for his diplomatic efforts with Afghanistan, China, Germany, and the United States.

Back in the Soviet Union, however, people joked that they'd rather he had won the Nobel Prize for Economics. For some, Gorbachev's reform proved too much too fast. For others, such as Boris Yeltsin, the reform didn't happen fast or fully enough. Skeptical world business leaders did not invest in Soviet businesses. It was taking time and money for new businesses to flourish, and people grew more impatient. They were used to being fed and housed

by the government. Prices soared for basics like food and clothing. Crime rose, too.

While Gorbachev succeeded in bringing democratic elections to the Soviet Union, his movement eventually meant his own political defeat. Yeltsin was elected chairman of the Russian Republic's Parliament, and his power grew. There seemed to be two presidents, each calling different shots. Yeltsin gained more followers and, in June 1991, he became the first leader elected by the people in 10 centuries.

Yeltsin, too, would discover that Russian reform was a slow process. In the last years of the 20th century, Russia's economy mirrored Yeltsin's faltering personal health. However, more nations began investing in Russia's businesses and sending aid. Mikhail Gorbachev may have lost power, but democracy persevered in the former Soviet Union.

In 1991 Boris Yeltsin defeated Mikhail Gorbachev in the kind of democratic election Gorbachev himself had brought to the Soviet Union. Despite Yeltsin's impatience for reform, severe food shortages still existed.

As mentioned in Chapter 3, the impeachment process lost favor in England centuries ago. How then did the English people rid themselves of leaders who had lost the public's favor? A few English tried assassination. Even the beloved Queen Victoria outlived seven attempts on her life. Mountbatten, who had given India the good news of independence, lost his life via a bomb on his boat. When Princess Diana died in a car crash in Paris in 1997, rumors of assassination cast their webs over her death.

Forced abdication, or surrender of the throne, remained an option for a Parliament that disliked its monarch. In 1936, the adventurous and popular Edward VIII ascended to the throne after the conservative George V died. Edward wanted to marry a twice-divorced American woman named Wallis Simpson. (Actually, she was still married when he broke the news.) Parliament, led by Prime Minister Stanley Baldwin, gave Edward an ultimatum: give up Mrs. Simpson or give up the throne. Following his heart, Edward gave up his claim to the throne, married Wallis Simpson, and settled for the title of Duke of Windsor. The couple went into exile in France and the Bahamas, where he was appointed governor. The Act of Abdication passed through all stages of approval in Parliament in one day, December 11, 1936.

The power of prime ministers and their Parliaments continued to grow stronger after the American Revolution. The role of the monarchs and lesser royals became that of figureheads—symbols of the realm. But if prime ministers could wield such power, it was necessary for some kind of check to exist against them.

The prime minister, head of the majority party in the House of Commons, is responsible for proposing and shepherding legislation through Parliament and making sure the legislation is enacted in the country. If the prime minister's programs fail, Parliament can call for a vote of confidence, which will show the level of support the prime minister may or may not have. In modern times, prime ministers have not lost such votes. If the prime minister does lose, he or she has three options: (1) resign, (2) let the leader of the opposition party form a new government, or (3) ask the reigning monarch to dissolve the current Parliament and call for new elections. (Elections for the House of Commons are usually held every five years.)

When the military overthrows a government, the new group of leaders is called a *junta.* (The word *junta* has its roots in the Latin word for "to join.")

The *junta* usually selects a dictator to rule, often with a strict hand. Central and South American countries that have a long history of these violent *coups d'état* include Venezuela, Nicaragua, Guatemala, El Salvador, Honduras, and Panama.

In the 20th century, the United States involved itself in many of these political intrigues. An independent counsel (similar to Kenneth Starr) found that the United States illegally supplied money and arms to Nicaraguan rebels in the 1980s.

An independent counsel found that the U.S. had illegally supplied money and arms to Nicaraguan rebels like these Miskito Indian Contras during the 1980s.

Members of the House Judiciary Committee at a press conference during the Clinton impeachment inquiry. Pictured are (L-R) Richard Gephardt, Newt Gingrich, Dick Armey, and Henry Hyde.

CHAPTER **6**

Senators, How Say You?

FOLLOWING THE IMPEACHMENT OF President Clinton by the House of Representatives on December 21, 1998, members of Congress took their holiday break. Many senators traveled to their home states and asked citizens how they felt about the impeachment. The senators also kept in touch with each other over the break, sharing their opinions.

Senators and voters alike wondered whether, with 55 Republicans and 45 Democrats in the Senate, Republicans would gain enough votes to convict Clinton by a two-thirds majority. The Republicans needed to sway 12 Democrats to reach a total of 67 votes.

The Senate opened its trial of Clinton on January 7, 1999. Supreme Court Chief Justice William Rehnquist presided. The first order of business was to approve a plan for the trial. They could not decide whether or not to call witnesses—such as Monica Lewinsky—to testify in person in the Senate. After all, every senator had a copy of the

Starr Report and transcripts of the witnesses' testimonies, even Clinton's. The senators put off this decision for a while.

Twelve House managers, led by Henry Hyde—a Republican from Illinois—presented their case against Clinton. Discussing the evidence, the managers argued that the Senate should convict Clinton on two articles of impeachment: perjury and obstruction of justice. They invoked the words of past President Theodore Roosevelt: "No man is above the law and no man is below it." Representative James Sensenbrenner of Wisconsin added, ". . . Clinton decided to put himself above the law not once, not twice, but repeatedly." Hadn't Clinton admitted to the American people that he lied?

Clinton's team of lawyers, including David Kendall, Charles Ruff, and Cheryl Mills, presented their case. They argued that the articles were "far short of what the American people demand be shown and proven before their democratic choice [the election of Clinton] be reversed."

Then the senators questioned lawyers on both sides for several days. After voting not to dismiss the charges and not to have live witnesses, the Senate agreed to view sections of testimonies that Independent Counsel Kenneth Starr had videotaped the previous summer. February 9 through 12, the Senate deliberated privately to discuss their verdict. On February 12, Justice Rehnquist asked, "Senators, how say you?"

On the perjury charge, senators voted exactly along party lines. Fifty-five Republicans voted guilty; 45 Democrats voted not guilty. On the obstruction of justice charge, the vote was even: 50, guilty; 50, not guilty. Not only had Republicans failed to sway any Democrats, but some Republicans had broken from the party to vote not guilty on this second article.

While Andrew Johnson's margin of victory was only one vote, President Clinton enjoyed a slightly more comfortable margin. Ultimately, however, both votes resulted in the same decision: acquittal. According to polls, acquittal of President Clinton was what the majority of Americans wanted.

Senator Edward Kennedy, a Democrat from Massachusetts, had voted not guilty. "Clearly, the framers [of the Constitution] intended the House and the Senate to use the impeachment power cautiously, and not . . . for partisan political purposes."

Senator Jon Kyl, a Republican from Arizona, voted guilty on both charges. He said that Clinton abused his power and was still allowed to remain in office. Evoking the image of his state's Grand Canyon, Kyl said, "The lesson is corrosive. Like water dripping on a rock, it eventually makes a deep hollow in the American justice system."

In a televised address, President Clinton apologized again for the events triggering the impeachment. He thanked the American people for their support and asked everyone to "rededicate ourselves to the work of serving our nation and building our future together."

Conclusion

At the time of the Constitutional Convention in Philadelphia, Thomas Jefferson was serving as a diplomat in France. When he returned to America, he had concerns about some of the decisions made by the Constitution's framers. Jefferson asked George Washington the reason for establishing a House of Representatives *and* a Senate. Washington replied with a question of his own: "Why did you pour that coffee into your saucer?"

"To cool it," Jefferson answered.

"Even so," Washington said. "We pour legislation into the senatorial saucer to cool it."

Presidents Andrew Johnson and Bill Clinton must have felt relieved and thankful for that constitutional cooling effect.

As a direct result of the opposition to Kenneth Starr's actions in the Clinton impeachment inquiry, Congress checked the judicial branch by failing to renew the law allowing for independent counsels.

Our government's system of checks and balances is a major reason why most impeachments have not resulted in conviction and removal from office. The Senate can check the House of Representatives in the same way that the House can check the president. The judicial branch actually provided the first check against Clinton, by the attorney general's appointment of an independent counsel. Since many members of Congress felt that Kenneth Starr dug too far afield at a huge cost, Congress failed to renew the law allowing for independent counsels. In doing so just months after Clinton's acquittal, Congress checked the judicial branch.

Impeachment, defined in Article II, Section 4 of our Constitution, gives American citizens an important tool to check leaders who cannot or will not check themselves.

Glossary

Article of impeachment—One specific charge made against the accused person. Members of Congress can vote guilty or not guilty on each article.

Bribery—The act of giving or accepting bribes. A bribe is money or items given or promised in exchange for a wrongful act or political favor.

Coup d'état—A French phrase literally meaning a "blow to the state." The phrase describes a sudden takeover of the government.

Crime—An act committed against a law.

Democratic party—One of the two major political parties in the United States of America. Democrats believe in a strong central government.

Federalist party—A political party operating between 1789 and 1819. Led by John Adams and Alexander Hamilton, the Federalists pushed for the adoption of the Constitution and for a strong central government.

Impeachment—A formal accusation—similar to an indictment—of wrongdoing by a civil officer such as the president, vice president, or a judge. The House of Representatives votes to impeach the officer. The Senate holds the trial and acts as an impartial jury. The chief justice of the Supreme Court presides over the trial.

Junta—A group of conspirators, often military, who overthrow a leader.

Misdemeanor—An act of misbehavior; an act breaking a minor law.

Precedent—An act, statement, legal decision, or case that serves as an example or justification for a later action or decision.

Republican party—The current American political party was organized in 1854 to oppose the extension of slavery. It believes that a country's strength lies more with the states and individuals than with the central government. An earlier Democratic-Republican party, led by Thomas Jefferson, also advocated for states' and individuals' rights.

Subpoena—A written legal document ordering a person to appear in court to testify and/or to submit records for evidence.

Treason—A violation of allegiance to, or the betrayal of, a state or country.

Further Reading

Brant, Irving. *Impeachment: Trials & Errors.* New York: Alfred A. Knopf, 1972.

Coulter, Ann, *High Crimes and Misdemeanors: The Case Against Bill Clinton.* Washington, DC: Regnery Publishing, 1998.

Emery, Fred. *Watergate: The Corruption of American Politics and the Fall of Richard Nixon.* New York: Times Books, 1994.

Heaps, Willard A. *Assassination: A Special Kind of Murder.* New York: Meredith Press, 1969.

Hoffer, Peter Charles, and N. E. H. Hull. *Impeachment in America 1635–1805.* New Haven: Yale University Press, 1984.

Isikoff, Michael. *Uncovering Clinton: A Reporter's Story.* New York: Crown Publishers, 1999.

Morris, Richard B. *The Constitution.* Minneapolis, MN: Lerner Publications, 1985.

Trefousse, Andrew. *The Impeachment of a President: The Blacks and Reconstruction.* Knoxville, TN: University of Tennessee Press, 1975.

Zeifman, Jerry. *Without Honor: The Impeachment of President Nixon and the Crimes of Camelot.* New York: Thunder's Mouth Press, 1995.

Special Periodical Issues

The New York Times, February 13, 1999, has a comprehensive chronology of the Clinton case, a record of the senatorial vote, texts of the decision and president's statements, as well as quotes from a good number of senators.

Time, December 21, 1998, discusses the House vote to impeach President Clinton.

U.S. News & World Report, February 22, 1999, places the Clinton impeachment in historical context and gauges its effect on the American people.

Index

ABOUT THE AUTHOR: Pegi Deitz Shea is a poet and an award-winning author of children's books, including *The Whispering Cloth* and *Ekaterina Gordeeva*. She teaches writing at the Institute of Children's Literature and lives in Connecticut.

ACKNOWLEDGMENTS: The author thanks George Arthur Deitz for instilling a love of history. And thanks also to Rockville Public Librarians, true pathfinders.

SENIOR CONSULTING EDITOR Arthur M. Schlesinger, jr. is the leading American historian of our time. He won the Pulitzer Prize for his book *The Age of Jackson* (1945) and again for *A Thousand Days* (1965). This chronicle of the Kennedy Administration also won a National Book Award. Professor Schlesinger is the Albert Schweitzer Professor of the Humanities at the City University of New York, and has been involved in several other Chelsea House projects, including the REVOLUTIONARY WAR LEADERS and COLONIAL LEADERS series.

Picture Credits